HIDDEN PLACES

HIDDEN PLACES

FROM SECRET SHORES TO SACRED SHRINES

CLAUDIA MARTIN

amber
BOOKS

Published by Amber Books Ltd
United House
North Road
London N7 9DP
United Kingdom
www.amberbooks.co.uk
Instagram: amberbooksltd
Facebook: amberbooks
Twitter: @amberbooks

Copyright © 2022 Amber Books Ltd.

All rights reserved. With the exception of quoting brief passages for the purpose of review no part of this publication may be reproduced without prior written permission from the publisher. The information in this book is true and complete to the best of our knowledge. All recommendations are made without any guarantee on the part of the author or publisher, who also disclaim any liability incurred in connection with the use of this data or specific details.

ISBN: 978-1-83886-168-1

Project Editor: Michael Spilling
Designer: Keren Harragan
Picture Research: Terry Forshaw

Printed in China

Contents

Introduction	6
North and South America	8
Europe	74
Africa and the Middle East	142
Asia and the Pacific	168
PICTURE CREDITS	224

Introduction

A world away from the museums of Paris, the skyscrapers of New York or the busy beaches of the Mediterranean, intrepid travellers can find strange and wonderful places that are little visited and little known. There are the far-flung islands of the Pacific Ocean, where divers can have the teeming reefs all to themselves. There are the whitewashed mountain villages of Spain, shut off from the outside world by switch-backing, white-knuckle roads. There are the national parks of the thickly forested Congo Basin, where elephants splash and play in the baï wetlands. There are the forgotten fortresses of the Andean cloud forest and the glaciers of the Canadian Arctic, where only wolves and foxes are disturbed by the crack of calving ice. Even in our buzzing, constantly switched-on world, there are still secret places waiting to be discovered with the same rush of surprise and joy as must have been felt by the travellers of long-past centuries: the overgrown temple ruins in the Cambodian jungle, the lava-choked church in central Mexico, the wind-worn arch in the Jordanian desert.

ABOVE:
Symi, Greece
Reached by ferry from Athens or the island of Rhodes, the Greek island of Symi surprises arrivals with its elegant Neoclassical port.

OPPOSITE:
Gili Meno, Indonesia
Little visited by tourists, tiny, car-free Gili Meno offers unspoilt reefs and golden beaches.

North and South America

The Americas are famed for their dazzling natural wonders, from vertiginous canyons to towering mountain ranges, from glaciers to teeming rainforests, from deafening waterfalls to deserts. While crowds throng the finest overlooks at the Grand Canyon and Niagara Falls, there are sites along less-travelled roads where nature's wildness offers at least as great a thrill. This region's far north and south are home to creeping glaciers and a wilderness of tundra, where visitors must camp beneath the stars or find lodging in isolated outposts built by trappers, loggers or whalers. Across the interior of this vast continent, the endless movement of tectonic plates, water and wind have worked their magic, conjuring geysers and travertine terraces, sand seas and sinkholes, buttes and windows. This slowly changing landscape has been inhabited for at least 15,000 years, during which time humans have also left their mark. Far from the well-known landmarks of New York and San Francisco, Rio de Janeiro and Mexico City, travellers can search for desert pueblos and cloud forest fortresses, for lava-wrapped villages and flood-threatened stilt houses. Even some of humankind's careless behaviour has been rendered beautiful on this continent, on the beaches scattered with glinting sea glass and brave flowers. Yet our behaviour is also threatening countless American species of animals and plants, making a journey to hear the call of a squirrel monkey or to watch a resting elephant seal ever-more precious and precarious.

OPPOSITE:
Montreal Botanical Garden, Canada
Founded in 1931 and designed by landscape architect Henry Teuscher, these botanical gardens house 22,000 species of plants, including a Wollemi pine, often called the world's rarest tree. The First Nations area of the garden showcases plants endemic to Quebec as well as medicinal and food plants of the First Nations.

ABOVE AND OPPOSITE:
Thomas Fisher Rare Book Library, Toronto, Canada
Canada's largest repository of rare books holds more than 15 million items, including Babylonian cuneiform tablets, Shakespeare's First Folio, Newton's *Principia*, papers belonging to Margaret Atwood and Leonard Cohen, and a collection of 500 19th-century Valentine cards. The rare book library shares a 1973 brutalist building with the Robarts Library. Designed by Mathers & Haldenby Architects, the concrete and steel structure has earned nicknames such as Fort Book, due in part to its protruding window bays, which are reminiscent of bartizans, the overhanging turrets seen in medieval castles.

ALL PHOTOGRAPHS:
Axel Heiberg Island, Nunavut, Canada
Located in the Arctic Archipelago, Axel Heiberg is uninhabited except for the seasonal McGill Arctic Research Station, but the island can be visited on boutique cruises and wilderness camping expeditions. Around the size of Switzerland, Axel Heiberg has a polar desert climate, with an average temperature of -19.7°C (-3.5°F). A third of the land is permanently covered by ice, while the rest is largely barren ground, dotted with low shrubs and grasses.

Bove Island, Yukon, Canada
Bove Island was named after 19th-century Italian Arctic explorer Giacomo Bove, whereas the lake on which it lies, Tagish, is named for the Tagish First Nations people. It was Tagish miners who made the gold discovery that led to the Klondike Gold Rush of 1896–99, when thousands of prospectors travelled across this stormy lake by small boat.

Dawson City, Yukon, Canada

Yukon's second largest town was founded in 1897 by gold prospector Joseph Ladue, who staked a claim to the boggy ground at the mouth of the Klondike River and sold lots for up to $8,000. After six months, about 5,000 prospectors lived in Dawson. Today, it is home to around 1,570 people, some of them still making their living from gold mining.

Haida Gwaii, British Columbia, Canada
Haida Gwaii archipelago has been home to the Haida people for at least 12,000 years. Heavy rainfall and mild temperatures have nurtured temperate rainforest on the islands' sheltered eastern sides. Sitka spruce, western hemlock and western red cedars shelter the Haida Gwaii black bear, which is far larger than its mainland relatives.

LEFT AND ABOVE:
Bowen Island, British Columbia, Canada
Reached by a short ferry or water taxi ride from Horseshoe Bay in West Vancouver, Bowen Island is known as Nexwlélexm in the Squamish language. The island's hiking trails wind through secondary forest where blacktail deer wander, stopping off at coves where seals and otters are the only company.

ALL PHOTOGRAPHS:
Mount Revelstoke National Park, British Columbia, Canada
With 15–24m (50–80ft) of snowfall each winter, Revelstoke draws intermediate and advanced skiiers and snowboarders with its challenging tree runs and vast backcountry skiing. The park's ski resort offers the longest vertical descent of any resort in North America, over 1,700m (5,575ft). In spring and summer, hikers explore the park's subalpine wildflower meadows and one of the world's few inland temperate rainforests.

ALL PHOTOGRAPHS:
Squamish, British Columbia, Canada
Squamish lies on the Sea to Sky Highway, which travels along the shore of Howe Sound, North America's most southerly fjord, past the snowcapped peaks of the Pacific Ranges. Just outside Squamish, a cable car and suspension bridge (pictured right) provide dizzying panoramic views. The Squamish Nation were hunting and fishing here for generations before the logging and railroad town of Squamish emerged in the early 20th century.

LEFT AND ABOVE:
Kenai Fjords National Park, Alaska, USA
This national park protects the Harding Icefield, which at 1,813 sq km (700 sq miles) is the largest icefield lying entirely in the United States. The icefield spawns over 40 glaciers, including Exit Glacier (pictured left), which was renamed after providing the exit route for the first crossing of the icefield, in 1968. Aialik Glacier (pictured above) calves regularly into the Gulf of Alaska's Aialik Bay.

Thor's Well, Oregon, USA
Close to Cape Perpetua, Thor's Well is said to be bottomless, endlessly sucking away the Pacific Ocean. In truth, the sinkhole is around 6m (20ft) deep and formed when the roof of a sea cave collapsed. The churning, spraying hole is most dramatic – and most dangerous – at high tide, when the hole fills with water from below until it bubbles over, then the water streams back into the chasm.

LEFT AND ABOVE:
Burney Falls, California, USA
These falls on Burney Creek, a tributary of the Pit River, were declared the 'Eighth Wonder of the World' by President Theodore Roosevelt. The falls are fed by snowmelt in spring, making them most dramatic from April to October. Despite its icy temperature, the plunge pool is popular for catch-and-release flyfishing of rainbow, brown and brook trout.

ALL PHOTOGRAPHS:
Glass Beach, California, USA
The sea glass on Glass Beach is the result of many years of garbage dumping in the nearby city of Fort Bragg. Sea glass has been frosted and smoothed by the pounding of waves and rocks. Despite the nature of the sand, the dunes around Glass Beach are home to the endangered, yellow-flowering Menzies' wallflower.

ALL PHOTOGRAPHS:
Taos Pueblo, New Mexico, USA
A World Heritage Site, Taos Pueblo is one of the Eight Northern Pueblos, which are communities of Tiwa- and Tewa-speakers believed to be among the oldest continuously inhabited settlements in the United States. Taos is a multi-storey adobe complex that was built on both sides of the Rio Pueblo probably some time between 1000 and 1450. Before the arrival of Europeans, Taos was a place of trade between the Pueblo peoples and the Plains Tribes to the northeast. Originally, the pueblo had few windows or conventional doors, with the rooms reached through wooden ladders in square holes in the roof.

ALL PHOTOGRAPHS:
Fly Geyser, Nevada, USA
Located in the Hualapai geothermal flat, this geyser is created by groundwater being heated by magma, resulting in water and steam of 93°C (200°F) spraying constantly from the surface. The geyser is home to thermophilic archaea, which thrive in the hot, mineral-rich water and colour the rocks red, yellow and green.

ALL PHOTOGRAPHS:
Garden of the Gods, Colorado, USA
Within Colorado Springs city limits, this extraordinary public park features fins of red and pink sandstone and pale limestone. These layers of sedimentary rock were deposited horizontally but tilted upright by the same tectonic forces that created the Rocky Mountains. Weaknesses in the strata were eroded into the features we see today, including the Balanced Rock (pictured far right), which is – for now – still joined to its base.

ALL PHOTOGRAPHS:
Great Sand Dunes National Park, Colorado, USA
This national park protects North America's tallest sand dunes, up to 230m (750ft) high. The formation of the dunes took place over millions of years. First, sediment from the surrounding mountains was washed into lakes covering the valley floor. After the climate dried and warmed, causing the evaporation of the lakes, the exposed sand was blown into dunes by the prevailing southwesterlies.

Hamilton Pool Preserve, Texas, USA

Hamilton Pool was created thousands of years ago by the collapse of the bedrock covering an underground river. Stalactites still jut from the limestone ceiling, which is now cloaked with moss and maidenhair ferns. The overhang and surrounding cliffs are stippled by the gourd-shaped nests of a colony of cliff swallows.

Fishing Pier, Jekyll Island, Georgia, USA
Jekyll Island is one of the barrier islands known as the Golden Isles of Georgia, built over millions of years by sand deposition. While the wind-whipped eastern shore boasts wide, flat beaches, the inland side of the island is covered by tidal salt marsh. Here birdwatchers can spot shorebirds including boat-tailed grackles, willets, roseate spoonbills and royal terns.

OPPOSITE:
Glory Hole Falls, Ozark National Forest, Arkansas, USA
Reached by a 3.2-km (2-mile) trail that begins at a small parking area on Highway 16, Glory Hole Falls pours around 9m (30ft) through the roof of an overhang cave. The trail passes several other enchanting waterfalls and cascades along its muddy way through the forest.

LEFT:
Hawksbill Crag, Ozark National Forest, Arkansas, USA
Also known as Whitaker Point, this jutting rock offers panoramic views of the old-growth forest, where oak and hickory dominate. While the 4.7-km (2.9-mile) out-and-back hiking trail to the rock is fairly easy (although unsuitable for young children due to unfenced drops), the winding, steep dirt road to the trailhead can be tricky for two-wheel drives in wet weather.

ALL PHOTOGRAPHS:
Apostle Islands, Wisconsin, USA
In the southwestern reaches of Lake Superior, the 22 Apostle Islands are blanketed by coniferous forest and roamed by plentiful black bears. In winter, the wave-carved caves of Devils Island and Sand Island are decorated with frozen waterfalls and delicate icicles. In some years, the lake freezes solid enough for the Park Service to allow people to walk to the caves from Meyers Beach on the Wisconsin shore.

OPPOSITE:

Ik Kil Cenote, Mexico
Close to the Mayan city of Chichen Itza, this cenote was sacred to the Maya people, who used it for sacrifices to the rain god, Chaac. A cenote is a sinkhole formed by the collapse of limestone bedrock, exposing groundwater. There are at least 6,000 cenotes in the karst of the Yucatán Peninsula, many of them suitable for swimming and scuba diving.

LEFT:

Thunder Bay National Marine Sanctuary, Michigan, USA
This sanctuary protects the site of 116 shipwrecks in storm-lashed Lake Huron. The earliest known wreck, from 1849, was of the paddle steamer *New Orleans*. The latest dates from 1975, when the steel *Barge No.12* sank for unknown reasons. Thunder Bay shelters just a fraction of the lake's shipwrecks, which number over a thousand.

FAR LEFT:
Copper Canyon, Mexico
This network of canyons in the Sierra Madre Occidental was carved by six tributaries of the Rio Fuerte. The rock has a coppery shade, whereas its cloak of vegetation lends a verdigris tint, earning the canyon its name. The canyon floor has a tropical climate where figs and palms thrive, while Mexican douglas firs cover the upper slopes.

LEFT:
San Juan Parangaricutiro, Mexico
A half-buried church is all that remains of the village of San Juan Parangaricutiro in the state of Michoacán. In 1943, the eruption of the Parícutin volcano very slowly began to bury the village and its neighbours in lava and ash. The villagers evacuated safely. Due to the survival of its altar and tower, the church is now a place of pilgrimage.

ALL PHOTOGRAPHS:
Montserrat, Leeward Islands
The southern half of the island of Montserrat, surrounding the Soufrière Hills volcano, is an exclusion zone thanks to ongoing volcanic activity, which destroyed the island's capital and forced two-thirds of the population to flee between 1995 and 2000.

The volcano is closely watched by the Montserrat Volcano Observatory, while a new town and port have been developed on the northwestern coast. The island has several endemic endangered species, including the black-and-yellow-feathered Montserrat oriole, the snake-like Montserrat galliwasp and the giant ditch frog, also known as the mountain chicken.

RIGHT:
Semuc Champey, Guatemala
At Semuc Champey (meaning 'Where the River Hides' in Q'eqchi'), the Cahabón River passes through a series of stepped limestone pools before flowing under a natural limestone bridge. This limestone is travertine, built up by the precipitation of calcium carbonate from the water. Over time, the rim of each pool grows taller, deepening the turquoise water.

OPPOSITE:
Great Blue Hole, Belize
Around 318m (1,043ft) across, this sinkhole began to form between 153,000 and 15,000 years ago, when the area was above sea level. Groundwater eroded a cave in the limestone bedrock. As the ocean rose, the cave flooded and its roof collapsed. Divers can admire the cave's stalactites, as well as sharks including the Caribbean reef shark, bull shark and great hammerhead.

ABOVE:
Suriname River, Suriname
The Suriname River flows from the Guiana Highlands, past the capital, Paramaribo, to the Atlantic Ocean at the Braamspunt sandspit. The river is known for species such as largetooth sawfish, spectacled caimans, peacock bass and redeye piranhas, all of which can be seen on kayaking and camping trips.

RIGHT:
Lençóis Maranhenses National Park, Brazil
In the rainy season, the valleys between the dunes of this vast sand sea fill with rainwater, which is prevented from draining by the impermeable bedrock. The interconnecting lakes are home to species such as the wolf fish, or trahira, which burrows into wet mud and remains dormant during the dry season.

ALL PHOTOGRAPHS:
São Salvador da Bahia, Brazil
Founded in 1549, Salvador was Brazil's first colonial capital and one of the world's first planned cities, overseen by Portuguese engineer Luís Dias. The city's historic centre, Pelourinho (pictured far right), is home to the blue 18th-century Church of the Third Order of Our Lady of the Rosary of the Black People, which was built by Brazilians of African descent.

ABOVE:
Madidi National Park, Bolivia
The black-capped squirrel monkey is found in the upper Amazon Basin, where it usually lives in female-dominated troops. These monkeys are extremely vocal, making a range of 'pips' for attention or alarm, 'chucks' to maintain communication in the dense forest and aggressive 'barks'.

RIGHT:
Madidi National Park, Bolivia
This diverse 18,958 sq km (7,320 sq mile) national park ranges from the glaciers of the Andes Mountains to tropical rainforest around the Tuichi River, from dry montane forest to the Yungas, an ecoregion of moist broadleaf forest. The park hosts around 120,000 species of insects.

RIGHT:
Salar de Uyuni, Bolivia
High in the Andes Mountains, Salar de Uyuni is the world's largest salt flat, covering over 10,000 sq km (3,900 sq miles). The flat formed as salt lakes evaporated from this dry plateau, which has no drainage outlets. A thick salt crust covers an immense pool of brine.

FAR RIGHT:
Tupiza, Bolivia
At an elevation of 2,850m (9,350ft), the city of Tupiza is ringed by high red sandstone escarpments, heavily eroded by rainfall and extremes of temperature. It is believed that outlaws Butch Cassidy and the Sundance Kid were killed nearby by the Bolivian army in 1908.

ALL PHOTOGRAPHS OVERLEAF:
Iquitos, Peru
In the Belén District of Iquitos, in the floodplain of the Itaya River, many of the homes float on rafts or are built on stilts to withstand the fluctuations of the river, which rises 5–6m (16–20ft) from February to July. The area has become a trading post, with goods such as charcoal, bananas and fish brought by canoe for sale in the city.

OPPOSITE:
Kuélap, Peru
On a ridge overlooking Utcubamba Valley, the city of Kuélap was built in the 6th century by the Chachapoyas culture. This civilization ruled a region of Andean cloud forest until, despite much resistance, it was conquered by the Inca in the 15th century. Kuélap's exterior wall, 18m (60ft) high, protected 400 buildings, many of them circular.

LEFT:
Punta Arenas, Chile
On the Strait of Magellan, Punta Arenas is one of the world's most southerly ports and also home to the world's most southerly Hindu temple, which is used by the Sindhi community. Much of the city's population has its roots among European colonists, particularly Croatians, who arrived in the mid-19th century. The central Barrio Croata offers many excellent Croatian-style restaurants.

OPPOSITE:
Nahuel Huapi National Park, Argentina
Argentina's oldest national park is centred on the glacial lake of Nahuel Huapi, but also encompasses glacier-capped peaks, Patagonian steppe and Valdivian temperate rainforest. On the southern shore of the lake is the town of Bariloche, known for its chocolate shops and Alpine-style architecture.

ABOVE:
Valdes Peninsula, Argentina
Jutting into the Atlantic Ocean, the Valdes Peninsula is largely barren land punctuated by salt lakes. Nevertheless, rheas, maras and guanacos can be spottted here. The peninsula is a breeding colony for southern elephant seals, while southern right whales mate in sheltered bays between May and December.

RIGHT:
Serranía de Hornocal, Argentina
In the valley known as Quebrada de Humahuaca, 150km (90 miles) north of Salta, are the bright, zigzagging formations of the Hornocal Mountains, formed of layers of sedimentary rock, tilted and folded by plate movements. This valley was a caravan route for Inca tradespeople, while evidence of hunter-gatherers dates back 10,000 years.

FAR RIGHT:
Quebrada de Cafayete, Argentina
The Quebrada de Cafayete lies along the road between Cafayete and Salta, with the formation known as Las Ventanas ('The Windows') around 10km (6 miles) east of Cafayete. This area of fins and arches was weathered and eroded by the forces of wind, water and extremes of temperature.

Europe

In the densely populated continent of Europe, it may be a surprise that any destination could still be considered a secret. Yet, even here, there are rarely visited mountain villages, hidden coves, empty hiking trails and turquoise glacial lakes where birds are the only company. Stranger still are the unexpected destinations that Europe offers for activities. While most surfers flock to Biarritz or San Sebastian, few journey to Norway's beautiful Lofoten Islands, where a small, thriving surfing community makes full use of modern wetsuit technology. While the warm, busy waters of the Mediterranean attract countless scuba divers, few travel to Iceland to dive among its rifts and hydrothermal chimneys. The sounds and straits of Scotland's rugged Inner Hebrides offer a dramatic alternative to sailing among the Greek Islands, while rafting on Montenegro's Tara River is as wild as anything France's Ardèche provides. Paragliders can soar among the thermals of Italy's Lake Garda, while walkers can explore the ravines of Romania's Nera Gorge-Beusnita National Park, while staying on the lookout for grey wolves and brown bears. Those in search of relaxation can wallow in the bathhouses of Tbilisi, less famous but no less ornate than the baths of Budapest. Wine-lovers can sample well-aged vintages in the world's largest wine cellars, in Moldova. Far from Venice, canals can be explored in London's Little Venice. Hundreds of miles from the Netherlands, windmills can be watched on the Estonian island of Saaremaa.

OPPOSITE:
Silfra Rift, Þingvellir National Park, Iceland
This fissure, in Þingvallavatn Lake, lies on the divergent boundary between the North American and Eurasian Plates. Every year, the plates move another 2 cm (0.8 in) farther apart, causing earthquakes, cracks and fissures. Scuba divers and snorkellers can explore the clear, meltwater lake, which remains around 2–4°C (36–39°F) year round.

Reine, Lofoten Archipelago, Norway
The fishing village of Reine is on the glacier-carved island of Moskenesøya. Despite lying above the Arctic Circle, the Lofoten Islands have mild winters due to warming by the North Atlantic Current. In recent years, the islands have become a surfing destination, particularly around Unstad Beach on Vestvagoy.

ALL PHOTOGRAPHS:
Svalbard, Norway
The Arctic archipelago of Svalbard has seven national parks, protecting mountains and fjords, glaciers and tundra, where polar bears, Arctic foxes and Svalbard reindeer can be seen.

Here, a group of snowmobiles cross the ice outside Longyearbyen, the largest settlement on Spitsbergen island. Spitsbergen is known for its quirky but necessary laws, such as that anyone walking outside must carry a rifle for protection against polar bears.

ABOVE:
Saksun, Streymoy, Faroe Islands
Traditional Faroese homes are constructed from the materials the islands have to offer: stone and turf, with the addition of occasional driftwood. Homes are built low to the ground, their living spaces partly dug from the earth, to offer insulation and protection from the wind.

RIGHT:
Tórshavn, Streymoy, Faroe Islands
The capital of the Faroe Islands, Tórshavn is home to around 19,000 people. It is said that Viking settlers first held their *ting* (parliament) on the Tinganes peninsula (pictured in the centre) in 825. The building closest to the flagpole is the government's main building today.

OPPOSITE:
Stockholm Archipelago, Sweden
This archipelago consists of 24,000 islands and islets, which were home to farmers and fishermen until the second half of the 20th century. Today, most of the archipelago's properties are used as holiday homes, although the islands closest to Stockholm have become popular with commuters. Summer visitors can swim, kayak, bike, hike and forage.

LEFT:
Saaremaa Island, Estonia
Estonia's largest island is known for its many windmills. Until the mid-20th century, most large farms here possessed a working mill for grinding their own flour. Today, Saaremaa draws domestic visitors with its juniper forests, medieval villages and wide sandy beaches where grey and ringed seals can be seen.

Maol-Bhuidhe,
Cape Wrath Trail, Scotland
This bothy, south of Loch Calavie, is one of the most remote habitable dwellings in Scotland. It is left unlocked and ready to use by hikers. Running through the Highlands for 330 km (205 miles) from Fort William to Cape Wrath, the Cape Wrath Trail is one of the United Kingdom's most challenging and rewarding walks.

LEFT:
Sound of Jura, Scotland
Between the Isle of Jura and the Scottish mainland, this sound is notoriously treacherous, with its skerries, strong tidal currents and the powerful Corryvreckan whirlpool, said to have been the end of Norse king Breacan. Yet sailing among the Inner Hebrides, its narrow harbours and sea lochs, is an unforgettable adventure for seasoned yachtspeople.

OPPOSITE:
Torc Waterfall, Killarney National Park, Ireland
This 20-m (66-ft) waterfall is formed where Owengarriff River drains from the corrie lake known as Devil's Punchbowl, at the base of Torc Mountain. The mountain takes its name from the Irish for 'wild boar'. Legend has it that Irish warrior Fionn Mac Cumhaill killed a magical boar on the mountain with his golden spear.

Glanmore Lake, Beara Peninsula, Ireland
Numerous hiking trails thread their way through the rugged, mountainous Beara Peninsula, including the 206-km (128-mile) circular Beara Way. This trail winds past megalithic stone circles and ring forts, fishing villages and whitewashed pubs, taking in views of coast and country.

ABOVE:

Glens of Antrim, Northern Ireland
The nine Glens of Antrim stretch from the Antrim Plateau to the coast of the North Channel ('Sruth na Maoile' in Gaelic). The valleys are farmed, but the uplands are carpeted in moorland and blanket bog. The valleys were carved by glaciers during the last Ice Age.

OPPOSITE:

Holkham Beach, England
On Norfolk's north coast, Holkham National Nature Reserve encompasses Holkham Beach's wide and windy foreshore, as well as salt marshes, woodland and sand dunes. The dunes are bound by marram grass, lyme grass and red fescue, as well as the rarer petalwort, bee orchid and carline thistle.

RIGHT:
Little Venice, London, England
Near Warwick Avenue tube station, at the junction of the Grand Union Canal, Regent's Canal and Paddington Basin, is a triangular pool where hundreds of houseboats have permanent moorings. Nearly twice the length of Amsterdam's canal network, London's canals are a part of Great Britain's 8,000 km (5,000 miles) of navigable canals and rivers.

OPPOSITE:
Osea Leisure Park, Blackwater Estuary, England
Essex's Blackwater River meets the North Sea at Mersea Island. The estuary holds the remains of V-shaped wood and wattle fish weirs dating from Saxon times, around 600 to 800 CE. At the head of the estuary is Maldon, known for its sea salt and annual mud race across the exposed riverbed.

LEFT:
Hérisson Waterfalls, France
In the Jura Mountains, between Doucier and Bonlieu, the Hérisson River plunges over no fewer than 31 waterfalls. A fairly well-marked 8.4-km (5.2-mile) path, following a section of the GR 559 long-distance footpath, passes through the river gorge. The highest falls, Cascade de l'Eventail (pictured), has a total drop of 65m (213ft).

RIGHT:
Colmar, France
The Alsatian city of Colmar is known for its Petite Venise quarter, where canals of the Lauch River crisscross the old tanner's, butcher's and fishmonger's neighbourhood. The half-timbered houses are painted in bright shades, which in medieval times revealed the trade of their inhabitants. Since those days, Colmar has been the centre of the Alsatian wine industry.

LEFT:

Men Ruz Lighthouse, Côte de Granit Rose, France

The 'Pink Granite Coast' stretches for 30 km (18 miles) along Britanny's northern shore. It is known for the warm shade of its sandstone, which has been eroded into stacks, windows and misshapen boulders as if it were butter. The lighthouse of Men Ruz takes its name from the Breton words for 'red stone'.

RIGHT:

Dune of Pilat, France

Around 106m (348ft) tall and 2.7km (1.7 miles) long, the Dune of Pilat is Europe's tallest sand dune. It is composed of sand deposited by sea breezes onto the vegetated shore. The dune offers views over the Landes pine forest, Arcachon Bay and the Banc d'Arguin sandbank, home to a nature reserve that protects migratory birds.

OPPOSITE:
Lac du Salagou, France
This reservoir was created in the 1960s to irrigate surrounding farmland and steady the water level of the Lergue and Hérault rivers. Locals have given the name *ruffes* (from the Occitan *rufa*, meaning 'red') to the rust-red banks and undulating mounds around the lake. The *ruffes* are formed of iron-rich claystone.

LEFT:
Nonza, Corsica, France
The village of Nonza is crowned by its stone tower, built as part of a coastal defence system by the Republic of Genoa, some time between 1530 and 1617. Nonza is on the west coast of the rocky peninsula of Cap Corse, where narrow roads wind past lemon groves and vineyards to vertiginously sited fishing villages.

RIGHT:
Cueva de los Verdes, Lanzarote, Spain
This network of lava tubes formed around 4,000 years ago after an eruption of La Corona volcano. The surface of the lava stream cooled and hardened, while the lava beneath flowed away, leaving the crust as the cave roof. The lava tubes extend for around 7.5 km (4.7 miles), both above and below the ocean, the latter portion forming the world's longest submarine lava tube.

OPPOSITE:
Orbaneja del Castillo, Spain
About an hour's drive north of Burgos, the village of Orbaneja del Castillo is known for its Romanesque architecture and its waterfall. The stream originates in a spring in the Cueva del Agua west of Orbaneja, runs through the village, then cascades over a series of algae-covered steps before meeting the Ebro River.

ALL PHOTOGRAPHS:
Parc del Laberint d'Horta, Barcelona, Spain
On Barcelona's western edge, this garden takes its name from its hedge maze. At the entry to the maze, there is a marble bas-relief of Ariadne and Theseus, who killed the Minotaur in a labyrinth created by Daedalus, navigating with the help of a ball of thread. Work on the garden began in 1791 at the request of the landowner, Marquis Desvalls.

ALL PHOTOGRAPHS:
Zuheros, Spain
In Córdoba province, Zuheros is one of this mountainous region's *pueblos blancos* ('white villages'), named for their whitewashed buildings. The first castle on the village's crag was built in the 9th century, but the current fortification dates from the 11th century, when the area was ruled by the Zirid Dynasty, who originated from the region of Algeria. The village is reached by a narrow road with many hairpin bends, which keeps away the majority of tourists.

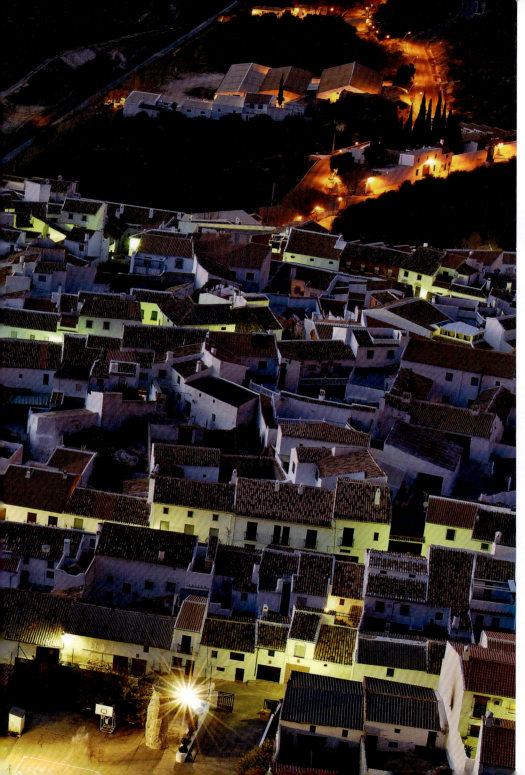

LEFT:
Algar do Carvão, Azores, Portugal
This cave on the island of Terceira is a vent in the dormant Guilherme Moniz volcano. With its entrance 583m (1,913ft) above sea level, the main cavern is reached down a moss-covered vertical passage, descended by steep and slippery stairs. Deep inside is a sulphurous, rainwater-filled pool.

ABOVE:
Casa do Penedo, Portugal
Located between Celorico de Basto and Fafe in the northern Portuguese district of Braga, this house was built in 1972–4, using four large boulders for portions of its walls and foundation. Despite being next to a wind farm, the house has no electricity supply.

ALL PHOTOGRAPHS:
Porto Santo, Madeira, Portugal
The island of Porto Santo formed over a hotspot in the mantle. On its southeastern coast, the Ana Ferreira peak has an 'organ pipe' formation (pictured left), its basalt columns created when a lava flow cooled differentially, shrinking and cracking into regular columns. The small island is known for its vineyards and long, golden-sand beach, Praia do Porto Santo. At the southern end of the beach is Ponta da Calheta (pictured right), where the volcanic rock has been sculpted by the waves.

OPPOSITE:
Fort of São Joao Baptista, Berlengas, Portugal
The uninhabited Berlengas Islands lie 10–17 km (6–11 miles) off the western coast of Portugal. Construction of the São Joao Baptista Fort, on a small island linked to Berlenga Grande by a causeway, was begun in the 17th century, since which time it has survived attacks by Barbary Coast pirates as well as Spanish and French troops.

LEFT:
Poca da Dona Beija, Azores, Portugal
On São Miguel, the largest island in the Azores Archipelago, the Furnas geothermal zone has given birth to more than 30 hot springs and spurting geysers. The last eruption of the Furnas volcano took place in 1630. In the village of Furnas, several 19th-century spas offer relaxation in hot, iron-rich pools, as well as pelotherapy with mineral mud.

OPPOSITE:

Sant'Agata de' Goti, Italy
This town perches on a tuff ridge between two tributaries of the Isclero River. The town's castle was built by the Norman Drengot family in the 11th century, while the Romanesque Church of the Annunziata has striking frescoes of the Last Judgement. The town overlooks the Sannio wine region, known for its Falanghina and Aglianico grapes.

LEFT:

Gardens of Bomarzo, Italy
Often called 'Park of the Monsters', these gardens were commissioned by Vicino Orsini in 1547, with the Mannerist sculptures created by Simone Moschino. Mannerism was a reaction to the harmony of High Renaissance art. The sculptures here include representations of the Roman god of the underworld, Orcus (pictured); a dragon; the multi-headed hound of Hades, Cerberus; and Hannibal's elephant.

ABOVE:
Malcesine, Italy
On the eastern shores of Lake Garda, Malcesine is squeezed between the lake's blue water and Monte Baldo. A cable car ascends the mountain, which is a destination for walkers, mountain bikers and, in winter, skiiers. Paragliders travel from afar to take advantage of the mountain's perfect thermals.

RIGHT:
Civita di Bagnoregio, Italy
The only way to reach the village of Civita di Bagnoregio is by a footbridge from the neighbouring town of Bagnoregio. The clay and tuff crag on which the village balances is prone to devastating erosion, earning the settlement the nickname of 'The Dying City'.

OPPOSITE:
Scala dei Turchi, Sicily, Italy
The 'Turkish Steps' is a sea cliff formed of the pale sedimentary rock marl, which is rich in carbonate minerals, clay and silt. Layers of the marl have been eroded at different rates, creating a step-like appearance. The 'Turkish' portion of the name derives from the raids by Saracens and Barbary pirates that this area experienced in the medieval and early modern period.

LEFT:
Rocca Calascio, Italy
This mountaintop fortress, or rocca, sits on a ridge above the Plain of Navelli, at a height of 1,460m (4,790ft). A single watchtower was constructed in the 10th century, but the current tower and courtyard were built in the 13th century to accommodate troops. After being badly damaged by an earthquake in 1461, the structure was never repaired.

Lauterbrunnen, Switzerland
Overlooked by the Eiger and Jungfrau, the village of Lauterbrunnen lies at the bottom of a deep, U-shaped valley, less than 1km (0.6 miles) wide. To the west of the village, Staubbach Falls plunges 297m (974ft) from a hanging valley. In 1779, Johann Wolfgang von Goethe wrote his poem 'Song of the Spirits over the Waters' after visiting the falls.

RIGHT:
Trümmelbach Falls, Switzerland
In the Lauterbrunnen Valley, Europe's largest subterranean waterfall system comprises ten falls that plunge through chasms inside a mountain ridge. The falls carry up to 20,000 l (5,280 gallons) of water every second, draining the glaciers of the Jungfrau, Mönch and Eiger. Visitors view the falls by taking a lift inside the mountain.

OPPOSITE:
Rakotzbrücke, Germany
This bridge in Gablenz is often known as Teufelsbrücke ('Devil's Bridge'), due to the folk belief that such miraculous bridges must have had a helping hand from Satan. Built in 1860, the bridge was designed to create a circle when reflected in the water beneath. The abutments are decorated with basalt columns, carved to appear as if formed naturally from the cracking of cooling lava.

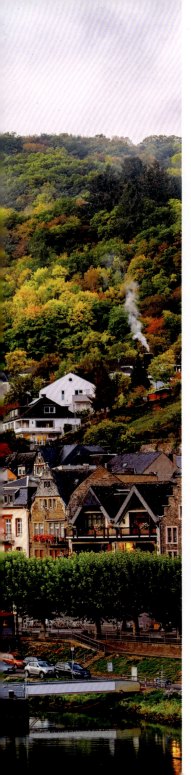

LEFT:
Cochem, Germany
On the banks of the Moselle, the town of Cochem is watched over by its castle, which was first built in the 11th century. In 1689, the castle was blown up by French troops during the Nine Years War. After being purchased by a wealthy businessman in 1868, it was rebuilt in Gothic Revival style.

ABOVE:
Freudenberg, Westphalia, Germany
Freudenberg's old town, Alter Flecken, consists of remarkably homogeneous 17th-century half-timbered houses, which date back to rebuilding works by John Maurice of Nassau after a fire in 1666. Many homes display the 'wild man' timber frame design, with the beams forming back-to-back 'K' shapes.

Crooked Forest, Gryfino, Poland

This pine grove of 400 trees was planted in around 1930. A few centimetres above each tree's roots, the trunk bends northwards, then slowly curves back to the vertical. No one is entirely sure how this happened, but the most logical explanation is that the trees' growth was distorted by foresters to create curving timber for boat-building or furniture-making.

RIGHT:
Stary Rynek, Poznan, Poland
On Poznan's Old Market Square, the Town Hall was built in the Mannerist style by architect Giovanni Battista di Quadro in 1550–60. The front, central tower features mechanized billy goats, which emerge from a door above the clock and butt heads daily at noon. To the left of the town hall is a row of 16th-century merchants' houses that were once home to fishmongers.

OPPOSITE:
Seegrotte Hinterbrühl, Austria
Europe's largest underground lake, with a surface area of 6,200 sq m (66,736 sq ft) is in a gypsum mine that closed in 1912 due to flooding. During World War II, the upper portions of the mine were used to construct Heinkel He 162A fighter jets for Nazi Germany, using forced labour from Mauthausen concentration camp.

LEFT:
Postojna Cave, Slovenia
Around 24 km (15 miles) long, this limestone cave system was eroded by the Pivka River. In 1872, a train began to carry tourists through the caves, which were later illuminated in 1884 by electric lighting, beating the capital, Ljubljana, to this modern convenience. Postojna is known for its fine speleothems, including flowstones and draperies.

RIGHT:
Vipava Valley, Slovenia
The mild climate of the Vipava Valley is suited to viticulture. Many of the finest wines are white, with grapes including the indigenous varieties Vitovska, Zelen and Pinela. These wines can be sampled alongside local sweet treats such as *štruklji* (rolled dumplings stuffed with walnuts, raisins and cottage cheese) and cherry strudel.

Đurđevica Tara Bridge, Montenegro
Built in 1940, a concrete arch bridge crosses the Tara River Canyon, the longest canyon in Europe at 78km (48 miles). The bridge's widest span, 116m (381ft) across, is used for bunjee jumping. From April to October, rafting trips along the Tara River, ranging from one- to three-day excursions, take in rapids, waterfalls, beaches and caves.

OPPOSITE:
Lake Koman, Albania
This lake was created in 1985–6 by damming the Drin River. The ferry that crosses the lake between the villages of Koman and Fierzë has been described as one of the world's best boat journeys. Locals, animals and occasional foreign visitors are treated to breathtaking views of peaks and gorges.

LEFT:
Agios Nikolaos, Crete, Greece
At the heart of Agios Nikolaos is Lake Voulismeni, which is connected to the harbour by a channel dug by the French in 1907. The lakeshore is lined with cafés and restaurants, where visitors can try specialities such as *dakos* (bread soaked with olive oil and topped with tomatoes and feta), washed down with raki.

Symi, Greece
Part of the Dodecanese island group, the island of Symi may take its name from the nymph Syme, who according to the ancient Greek author Athenaeus was carried off by the sea god Glaucus. Many of the port's 19th-century buildings are in the Neoclassical style, with pediments decorated with a central 'ox eye' window for ventilation.

RIGHT:
Nera Gorge-Beusnita National Park, Romania
In the Anina Mountains, this national park is home to brown bears, grey wolves, wild boars, European wildcats and golden eagles. The park is also known for its karst lakes and many waterfalls, including pretty Vaioaga Falls, which is reached by a short hike from the very potholed road.

FAR RIGHT:
Clay Castle of the Valley of the Fairies, Romania
This ecofriendly building was constructed from clay, sand, stone and straw, drawing both from the world of fairytales and the Transylvanian Gothic style. Although intended to be a hotel, the castle is functioning as an attraction with an organic restaurant. The surrounding Transylvania Plateau offers hikes through farmland, ravines and canyons.

FAR LEFT:
Transfagarasan Highway, Romania
Closed by snow between late October and June, this switch-backing road climbs to 2,042m (6,699ft) in the Fagaras Mountains, giving access to the lovely glacier lake of Bâlea. The road was built by military personnel from 1970 to 1974, during the rule of Nicolae Ceausescu. Official estimates put the number of deaths during construction at 40.

TOP AND BOTTOM LEFT:
Milestii Mici, Moldova
The Milestii Mici winery has the world's largest wine cellar, which stores nearly 2 million bottles in tunnels created by a disused limestone mine. The caverns extend for 200km (124 miles), but only 55km (34 miles) are in use by the winery. The most expensive bottles here are a 1973 dessert wine that sells for over £1,000.

Tbilisi, Georgia
The architecture of Georgia's capital reflects its long and varied history, with Byzantine buildings beside delicate Art Nouveau and rigid Stalinist structures. On a crag overlooking the city is the Narikala fortress, first built as a Persian citadel in the 4th century. Nearby are several sulphur bathhouses, housed in lavish, ornately tiled buildings.

Africa and the Middle East

Studded by vast deserts, rainforests, savannas and wetlands, Africa and the Middle East draw visitors from across the world with their natural marvels. Many of these visitors long to see the Big Five: the lion, leopard, black rhinoceros, African bush elephant and African buffalo, all except the last of these extraordinary animals threatened by hunting and habitat loss. Every year, nearly 1 million people make a trip of a lifetime to South Africa's beautiful Kruger National Park, while hundreds of thousands more reach Kenya's Maasai Mara and Tanzania's Serengeti National Park. Yet for those willing to travel a little further, walk a little deeper, perhaps sleep a little rougher, the fauna of other, lesser-known national parks awaits, including the spotted hyenas and forest elephants of the Congo's Odzala-Kokoua, the mountain gorillas of Rwanda's Volcanoes National Park, or the lions, cheetahs, hippos and giraffes of Tanzania's Selous. Even farther off the beaten track, the rainforested islands of São Tomé and Príncipe are home to an extraordinary collection of endemic plants and animals, including towering begonias and small, shy tree frogs. Only around 300 km (186 miles) from the west African coast, these islands see no more than 13,000 visitors a year. Almost as overlooked are Mozambique's Quirimbas Islands, where a pristine national park protects marine wildlife ranging from rarely seen dugongs to critically endangered hawksbill turtles, from well-camouflaged circular batfish to fast-swimming rainbow runners.

OPPOSITE:

Jabal al Kharaz, Wadi Rum, Jordan
Weathered by extremes of temperature and eroded by wind, the sandstone arches of Wadi Rum may stand for only 20,000 years before they crumble into the red desert. In 1917–18, British army officer T.E. Lawrence travelled here, writing that the rock formations "gave the finishing semblance of Byzantine architecture to this irresistible place."

Wadi Rum, Jordan
This desert valley, covering 720 sq km (280 sq miles), was formed after layers of granite and sandstone were uplifted during the creation of the Great Rift Valley, more than 5 million years ago. The soft sandstone was eroded along cracks and fissures. In Arabic, *wadi* means 'dry valley', whereas *rum* may have its roots in the Aramaic word for 'high'.

ALL PHOTOGRAPHS OPPOSITE:
Leptis Magna, Libya
Founded by the Phoenicians in the 7th century BCE, Leptis Magna fell under Roman control after the defeat of Carthage in 146 BCE. The Roman emperor Septimius Severus was born in the city, leading to an extensive building programme and the construction of a triumphal arch (far left) on the occasion of his African tour in 203 CE.

LEFT:
Lixus, Morocco
The trading centre of Lixus, making its living from cloth, dye, wine and carvings in ivory and wood, was founded by the Phoenicians on the banks of the Loukkos River. Parts of the city were inhabited until the days of the Marinid Sultanate, in the 14th century, when the site was abandoned due to changes in the river's course.

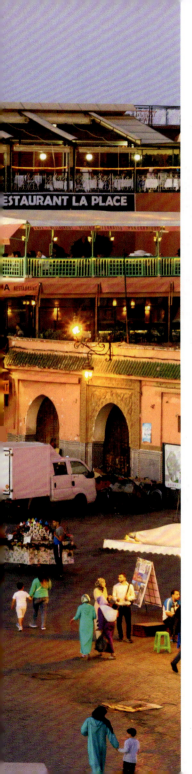

LEFT:

Jemaa el-Fnaa, Marrakesh, Morocco
The main square of Marrakesh's old city became the site of markets, festivals and executions soon after the city was founded by the Almoravids in 1070. The square's name may translate as 'Assembly of the Dead', perhaps a reference to those executions and perhaps to the deadly collapse of the nearby Koutoubia mosque in the 18th century.

ABOVE:

Jemaa el-Fnaa, Marrakesh, Morocco
Crowds gather in Jemaa el-Fnaa to hear the piping of snake charmers' *pungis* and the hypnotic call-and-response singing of Gnawa troupes, who beat rhythms with their *krakeb* cymbals (pictured). Acrobats leap, sad monkeys are led on chains and henna artists swirl patterns on the hands of visitors and locals. Countless food stalls sell specialities such as spiced snail broth.

ALL PHOTOGRAPHS:
São Tomé and Príncipe
The island country of São Tomé and Príncipe lies in the Gulf of Guinea. Cocoa is a major export, while home-grown coffee is used as a flavouring in savoury stews and snacks. There is a high degree of endemism among the islands' fauna, which includes the endangered São Tomé shrew, São Tomé free-tailed bat and São Tomé grosbeak.

ALL PHOTOGRAPHS:
Odzala-Kokoua National Park, Republic of the Congo
Around 100 mammal species are found in this national park in northwestern Congo. Primates include the western lowland gorilla (pictured) and central chimpanzee, as well as eight species of monkeys. There is a declining population of the critically endangered African forest elephant (pictured), which plays a major role in dispersing the tree species of this tropical moist broadleaf forest through its dung.

Volcanoes National Park, Rwanda
This national park encompasses five volcanoes, only one of which, Bisoke, is believed to be active. The park was the base for American naturalist Dian Fossey, who dedicated her life to the region's mountain gorillas. Up to 1.7m (5.6ft tall), this great ape lives in a stable, peaceful and highly vocal group of up to 30.

Fish River Canyon, Namibia
This ravine, 160km (100 miles) long and up to 549m (1,801ft) deep, was carved into the plateau by the Fish River. The river is a torrent in late summer, but spends the rest of the year as a chain of shallow pools. Although the region receives only around 6.8cm (2.7in) of rain a year, 1 sq km of land can be home to over 360 plant species.

ALL PHOTOGRAPHS:
Kafue National Park, Zambia
Zambia's largest national park, roughly the size of Wales, is covered by miombo woodland (open, semi-deciduous forest), interspersed with dambos grassland, which becomes marshy in the wet season. The park is known for its many species of antelope, including Lichtenstein's hartebeest (pictured), which gathers in herds of up to 15 females, led by 1 male.

Luangwa River, Zambia
The 770-km (478-mile) Luangwa River flows through North and South Luangwa National Parks, where mopane trees dot the grassy valley floor and miombo woodlands cloak the hills. The parks have large populations of African bush elephants, common hippos, Nile crocodiles, Thornicroft's giraffes, Crawshay's zebras and Cape buffaloes.

ALL PHOTOGRAPHS:
Selous Game Reserve, Tanzania
Covering 50,000 sq km (19,000 sq miles), the landscape of Selous ranges from grassland to acacia savanna to miombo woodland. Large predators include lions and wild dogs. The reserve is named after Victorian hunter and author Frederick Selous, whose stuffed lions made it into the collection of London's Natural History Museum.

ALL PHOTOGRAPHS:
Lake Natron, Tanzania
A salt lake in the Gregory Rift, Natron is fed by mineral-rich hot springs and the Southern Ewaso Ng'iro River. The lake's shallow, warm water, up to 60°C (140°F), is often covered by a salt crust. Salt-loving blue-green algae thrive here, fed on by lesser and greater flamingos.

LEFT:
Ibo, Quirimbas Islands, Mozambique
A colonial-era villa on Ibo island. Long home to fishermen, Ibo gained strategic importance as an Arab and, later, a Portuguese trading port. The island is known for its silversmiths, who work intricate jewellery inspired by Arab traditions and the Goan techniques brought by craftspeople who arrived in the 17th century.

RIGHT:
Matemo, Quirimbas Islands, Mozambique
Quirimbas National Park protects 1,430 sq km (550 sq miles) of coastal forest, mangroves and coral reef, which is home to 375 species of fish, including parrotfish, angelfish and long-nosed hawkfish. The islands' beaches are nesting sites for green and olive ridley turtles, while dugongs graze shyly in offshore seagrass meadows.

Asia and the Pacific

This vast region is home to many of the world's most visited and iconic attractions, with Australia's Great Barrier Reef, India's Taj Mahal and China's Forbidden City only three among many. Yet this region also rewards intrepid travellers with countless lesser-known sites that simply snatch the breath away with their pure beauty or their vaunting ambition. While 5 million people flock to Australia's Great Barrier Reef every year, few journey to the reefs of Rangiroa and Tuvalu, thousands of miles across the Pacific Ocean from almost anywhere. Once there, most swimmers will share the reef only with hundreds of species of fish, among them vivid parrotfish and squirrelfish, as well as sharp-sensed sharks and rays. One of Asia's other pre-eminent attractions, the Taj Mahal, is among the world's most recognizable buildings. Shah Jahan's mausoleum for his wife Mumtaz Mahal is visited by 8 million people every year. The white marble masterpiece is in the Mughal style, its blueprint created hundreds of years earlier by Shah Jahan's great ancestor, Timur. This conqueror's sublime, azure-tiled mausoleum, celebrating both the glory of God and human endeavour, is in less-visited Samarkand, a scholarly oasis in an arid region of Uzbekistan. Around 15 million visitors enter Beijing's Forbidden City each year, making it one of the world's most popular attractions. Less famous but equally imposing is the Forbidden City of Hue, Vietnam, which was also the home of a proud emperor, Gia Long, and his many wives, who led out their lives behind similarly austere walls and moats.

OPPOSITE:
Sangan Waterfall, Alborz Mountains, Iran
At an elevation of 2,700m (8,858ft), the dripping of Sangan Waterfall builds an ice stalagmite up to 40m (131ft) tall each winter. In spring, the waterfall flows once more due to melting of the Cheshme Shahi and Pahneh Hesar glaciers. Sangan is in the Central Alborz, close to Iran's highest peak, the 5,610-m (18,406-ft) stratovolcano Mount Damavand.

Darvaza Gas Crater, Turkmenistan

In the Karakum Desert a 69-m (226-ft) wide crater has been burning since 1971, earning it the nickname 'Door to Hell'. The most widely believed story concerning its provenance is that Soviet geologists were exploring this vast natural gas field when the ground beneath their drilling rig collapsed. They ignited the crater to stop the spread of methane gas – and it has burned ever since.

ALL PHOTOGRAPHS:
Gur-e-Amir, Samarkand, Uzbekistan
Thanks to its location on the Silk Road between China and Europe, Samarkand was one of Asia's largest cities by the 14th century, when the Turco-Mongol conqueror Timur made it his capital and, later, the site of his family mausoleum, Gur-e-Amir ('Tomb for the King'). This was a landmark of Central Asian architecture, inspiring many later tombs, including the Taj Mahal, which was built by one of Timur's descendants, Shah Jahan.

LEFT:
Iskanderkul, Tajikistan
Formed by a landslide that blocked the Saratogh River, this lake high in the Gissar Range is named after Alexander the Great (Iskander is the Persian pronunciation of Alexander, whereas *kul* means 'lake'). Legend tells us that Alexander (356–323 BCE) ordered the landslide to punish locals who resisted his rule.

ABOVE:
Garden of Caves, Laitmawsiang, India
In the northeastern Indian state of Meghalaya is the Garden of Caves, a fairytale place of waterfalls, springs, streams and open caves that is usually overlooked by visitors. Stone paths and stairways lead the winding way through the forest, revealing one delicate prospect after another.

ALL PHOTOGRAPHS:
Jaisalmer, India
Founded by Rawal Jaisal in 1156, Jaisalmer is known as the 'Golden City' due to the sandstone of its houses, temples and fort, which crowns Trikuta Hill. Temples, shrines, ghats (bathing wharves) and chhatris (dome-shaped pavilions) adorn the shore of the artificial Gadisar Lake, which was built to provide water to this desert-bound city.

ABOVE:
Pangong Lake, China–India
Around 134km (83 miles) long, Pangong crosses the line of control between China and India. Sandwiched between the Karakoram and Pangong ranges, the lake has no outflow, losing water only through evaporation and seepage. The eastern portion of the lake is fresh, whereas the west is saline.

RIGHT:
Jiuzhaigou National Park, China
In Sichuan Province, on the edge of the Tibetan Plateau, this national park protects a forest-covered karst landscape punctuated by glacial lakes and countless waterfalls. The park's fauna includes small and isolated populations of endangered giant pandas and golden snub-nosed monkeys.

ALL PHOTOGRAPHS:
Mount Sanqing, China
This sacred mountain's name means 'Three Pure Ones', in reference to its three summits, Yujing, Yushui and Yuhua, which symbolize the Taoist trinity, the three greatest gods in the pantheon. The mountain is home to many rare plants, including the Chinese douglas fir and countless bright rhododendrons.

ALL PHOTOGRAPHS:
Hitachi Seaside Park, Japan
Each spring, local people flock to this vast public park in the city of Hitachinaka to see the blooming of 4.5 million baby blue-eyes flowers (pictured left). Summer brings poppies, zinnias and sunflowers; autumn offers kochia and cosmos flowers; while winter is the turn of ice tulips. A small amusement park boasts a ferris wheel 100m (328ft) tall.

ALL PHOTOGRAPHS:
Shirakawa-go, Japan
The remote village of Shirakawa-go was constructed in the vernacular building style known as *gassho-zukuri* ('prayer-hands construction'), named for the steeply sloping roofs that easily shed heavy snowfalls. The upper floors of these wooden homes were traditionally used for sericulture, providing space for trays of silkworms and mulberry leaves.

ALL PHOTOGRAPHS:
Hinatuan Enchanted River, Mindanao, Philippines
This river gained its name from local myths of the *engkanto* (from the Spanish *encanto*, meaning 'enchanted') said to dwell in its unexplored depths. *Engkanto* are spirits, often associated with ancestors, that can appear in human form. One legend tells of *engkanto* that gave the river its extraordinary shades of sapphire and jade.

RIGHT:

Thiên Duòng Cave, Vietnam
In Phong Nha-Ke Bàng National Park, this 31-km (19-mile) limestone cave was discovered in 2005. The largest portion of the cavern, 150m (492ft) wide, is baroquely ornamented by stalactites and stalagmites, formed by the dripping of mineral-rich rainwater. In 2012, a new species of cave-dwelling scorpion was found here.

OPPOSITE:

Côn Dao, Vietnam
Much of the archipelago of Côn Dao, consisting of 16 mountainous islands and rocky islets, is protected as a national park. Endangered species here include the dugong and green turtle, which feed on seagrasses in the warm, shallow water. The critically endangered hawksbill turtle searches for sea sponges on the coral reef.

ALL PHOTOGRAPHS:
My Son, Vietnam
In a narrow valley in central Vietnam is a cluster of Hindu temples (most of which are dedicated to Shiva) dating from the 4th to 14th century. The valley was a burial place and site of religious ceremony for the Kings of Champa. More than 30 stone steles bear political and religious inscriptions. Many of the temples were damaged by US bombs during the Vietnam War.

Imperial City, Hue, Vietnam

Work on the walled citadel of Hue began in 1804, soon after Gia Long proclaimed himself first emperor of a unified Vietnam. The citadel, ringed by a moat 10 km (6 miles) long, contained the Imperial City, itself protected by a moat and wall 2.5km (1.6 miles) long. Within the Imperial City was the Forbidden City, the residences barred to all but the imperial family.

RIGHT:
Sambor Prei Kuk, Cambodia
The city of Sambor Prei Kuk was probably established as the capital of King Isanavarman I (ruled 616–637) of the Chenla Kingdom, when it was known as Isanapura. The ruined temples, palaces and reservoirs, constructed in sandstone and brick, are interspersed with lingams (phallic symbols of Shiva) and lion statues.

OPPOSITE:
Phnom Santuk, Cambodia
The sacred Buddhist mountain of Phnom Santuk is climbed by 809 steps that are flanked by statues of women (on the left) and men (on the right) holding a *naga* serpent (pictured). *Naga* represent a bridge between the mortal and immortal realms. On the hill's summit are five large rock-cut statues of the Buddha and several wats (temples) decorated with dragons.

Kuang Si Falls, Laos
The many-tiered Kuang Si Falls are formed of travertine, a type of limestone composed of calcium carbonate deposited by the shallow, mineral-rich water. The pale travertine reflects sunlight, resulting in the turquoise luminosity of the water. Fish in the pools offer a free spa treatment by nibbling at the dead skin on bathers' feet.

ALL PHOTOGRAPHS:
Wat Phra That Doi Suthep, Thailand
This Theravada Buddhist temple complex is located on a sacred mountain around 15km (9 miles) from the busy city of Chiang Mai. According to legend, the temple was founded in 1383 when a white elephant, carrying a relic of the Buddha, climbed to the top of the mountain, trumpeted three times, then fell to the ground, dead.

LEFT:

Wat Phra That Doi Phra Chan, Thailand

A half-hour's drive from Lampang, this spectacularly positioned temple was built in the traditional Lanna style of the eponymous kingdom, which ruled this region from the 13th to 18th century. The style is characterized by steeply pitched, multi-tiered roofs, with small windows and doors that let in little light.

RIGHT:

Hsinbyume Pagoda, Myanmar

The design of this white-painted pagoda is based on descriptions of the mythical Buddhist sacred mountain, Mount Meru, with seven rippling terraces representing the seven mountain ranges that surround Meru. The pagoda was ordered by King Bagyidaw in 1819, in honour of his first wife, Hsinbyume, who had died in 1812.

LEFT:
Aung Mingalar, Inle Lake, Myanmar
Myanmar is a country of countless stupas, more than 1,479 of them exceeding 8.2m (27ft) tall. Stupas are bell-shaped, tiered structures, often known as pagodas, that house sacred relics, including those associated with the Buddha and *arhats* (enlightened people).

ABOVE:
Inle Lake, Myanmar
Fishermen on Inle row standing up, controlling their oar with one leg and hand, allowing them to see down into the plant-filled water. This rowing style leaves the other hand and leg free to slam in a conical net to catch fish such as the endemic but endangered Inle carp, Sawbwa barb and Lake Inle danio.

ABOVE:
Rawa Island, Malaysia
Rawa is named after its many white doves, which flutter among this coral island's palms. Reached only by boat from the port of Mersing on the Malay Peninsula, the island has no roads, only walkways. Rawa's few visitors can snorkel among blacktip reef sharks, clownfish, angelfish and stingrays.

RIGHT:
Cameron Highlands, Malaysia
This tableland region of the Malay Peninsula is known for its tea plantations, most of them first planted in the 1930s. The majority of tea grown here is the large-leaved *assamica* variety, which is used mainly for black tea. Most of the country's 3.6 million kg (8 million lbs) of tea is drunk domestically.

Sama Village, Maiga Island, Malaysia
The Sama-Bajau are a marine nomadic people, who live by fishing and, today, by cultivating seaweed. Some live in stilt houses close to shore, while others sleep aboard wooden houseboats known as *lepa*. Dispersed across parts of Malaysia, Indonesia, the Philippines and Brunei, the Sama-Bajau speak languages in the Samana group of the Austronesian language family.

FAR LEFT:
Tiwu Ata Bupu, Flores Island, Indonesia
There are three crater lakes on the Kelimutu volcano, the colour of each lake changing regularly due to the level of elements such as manganese, the input of volcanic gas and rainfall. Ata Bupu (Lake of Old People) is usually blue, whereas Ko'o Fai Nuwa Muri (Lake of Young Men and Maidens) and Ata Polo (Enchanted Lake) are green or red.

LEFT:
Jomblang Cave, Indonesia
Entry to this cave system is by a combination of abseiling and scrambling, with (helmeted) visitors helped through the unforgettable adventure by teams of local people. After a further 280-m (920-ft) scramble along a slippery, dark path, visitors are rewarded by rays of sunlight shining through the collapsed sinkhole above, known here as 'heavenly light'.

ALL PHOTOGRAPHS:

Nusa Islands, Indonesia
Off the coast of Bali, Nusa Penida (far left) and Nusa Lembongan (left) provide an unofficial bird sanctuary where critically endangered birds, including the Bali myna and Java sparrow, are released into the wild after captive breeding. The islands are also renowned for their reefs, with large visitors including ocean sunfish, manta rays and numerous sharks.

RIGHT:
Suluban Beach, Bali, Indonesia
Bali's southern Pecatu region draws both surfers and nudists. Access to its Suluban Beach is down steep and winding stairs, then through a cave to the golden sand. Although the beach is usually quiet, its perfect waves attract professional surfers from across the world. The dry season, from May to October, offers the best conditions.

OPPOSITE TOP AND BOTTOM:
Gili Air, Indonesia
Off the coast of Lombok, the tiny island of Gili Air has forbidden motorized vehicles, so the only transport is by foot, bicycle and the small, bell-decorated, horse-drawn carriage known as a *cidomo*. Visitors can swim on the coral reef, which is visited by endangered green turtles and critically endangered hawksbill turtles.

RIGHT:
Carnarvon Gorge, Australia
In central Queensland, Carnarvon Gorge is significant to the Bidjara, Karingbal and Kara Kara peoples, the rock art on the gorge's sandstone walls testament to their long histories. Much of the work here is stencil art, created by blowing watery ochre pigment over an object held against the wall, such as a hand, boomerang, shield or axe. The gorge's oldest sites have been in use for over 3,000 years.

OPPOSITE:
Secret Falls, Tasmania, Australia
A short hike west of Hobart along the Myrtle Gully track is this 3-m (10-ft) waterfall. Plunging into a narrow gully and cloaked by undergrowth, Secret Falls is easy to miss. Hobart is at the intersection between temperate mixed forest and rainforest. Fern diversity is high, with species including soft tree fern and mother shield fern.

LEFT:
Little Beach, Nanarup, Australia
Around 8km (5 miles) east of Nanarup in Two People's Bay Nature Reserve, this beach is known for its limpid turquoise water and white sand. The nature reserve was established to protect the endangered noisy scrubbird, named for the male's territorial song, which starts pleasantly and ends earsplittingly.

ABOVE:
Gunlom Falls, Kakadu National Park, Australia
These falls cascade 85m (279ft) into a plunge pool, which is not recommended for swimming due to occasional estuarine crocodiles. The Jawoyn traditional owners tell how this landscape was created by Nabilil the Crocodile, who travelled from the sea, holding his *meya* (firestick).

ABOVE:

Rangiroa Lagoon, Tuamotu Islands, French Polynesia
Enclosed by an immense atoll, Rangiroa Lagoon has an area of 1,446 sq km (558 sq miles). Atolls are ring-shaped coral reefs formed by the subsidence of an island about which a fringing reef had formed. Marine life here includes hammerhead sharks, leopard rays, bottlenose dolphins and numerous reef fish.

RIGHT:

Tetamanu, Tuamotu Islands, French Polynesia
An island of the Fakarava atoll, Tetamanu is accessible only by private boat. Once here, visitors can visit the 19th-century coral chapel, which is surrounded by coral gravestones. This atoll protects one of the world's most pristine coral reefs, home to a school of around 700 grey reef sharks.

Tuvalu
With a population of around 10,500 people, the island country of Tuvalu comprises three coral islands and six atolls, with a land area of 26 sq km (10 sq miles). A traditional social system survives in part in Tuvalu, with each family supplying a particular *salanga*, or skill, such as fishing or house-building. Only a few hundred tourists visit every year.

Na Pali Coast, Kaua'i, Hawaii
Basalt cliffs rise to 1,200m (4,000ft) along Kaua'i's northwestern coast (in Hawaiian, Na Pali means "the cliffs"). Like all the Hawaiian islands, Kaua'i formed from lava as the Pacific Plate moved over a hotspot in the mantle. The battering of waves and heavy stream erosion, due to this region's high rainfall, have carved spines and ridges.

Picture Credits

Alamy: 12 (Design Pics Inc), 13 (Nature Picture Library), 53 (Keith Dannemiller), 54 (Robert Harding), 57 (Stephen Frink Collection), 61 (Cro Magnon), 62 (Nature Picture Library), 69 (Mauritius Images), 74 (Nature Picture Library), 62 (Paul Brown), 86 (Genevieve Leaper), 93 (Andrew Ray), 104 (Jam World Images), 108 (Eric Nathan), 109 (Kozlowski Premium RM Collection), 110 (Emmanuel Lattes), 111 (Kozlowski Premium RM Collection), 123 (Urbanmyth), 147 (Witold Shyrypczak), 153 (Danita Delimont), 166 (John Warburton-Lee Photography), 167 (Ariadne Van Zandbergen), 195 (Amnat), 206/207 (Hazize San), 208 (Loop Images Ltd), 216 (Michael Evans), 217 (Ingo Oeland)

Dreamstime: 6 (Emicristea), 7 (Wonderful Nature), 11 (Borisgelman84), 14/15 (Stephen Smith), 16/17 (Edgar Bullon), 24 (Sebastien Fremont), 25 (Colin Moore), 28/29 (Backyardphotography707), 32 (Maksershov), 35 (Josemaria Toscano), 40 (Brent Coulter), 44/45 (Nickolay Khoroshkov), 47 (Brandon Alms), 48 (Wisconsinart), 52 (Enrique Gomez Tamez), 55 (Alistairhomer), 56 (Marixtu22), 59 (A Sab), 64 (Davide Guidolin), 65 (Rafal Cichawa), 67 (Carlos Mora), 68 (Matyas Rehak), 70 (Eduardo Mariath), 71 (Pablo Caridad), 76/77 (Miroslav Liska),), 78 (Ondrej Prosicky), 79 (Tyler Olson), 91 (Ashley Taylor), 94 (Meinzahn), 97 (Janvw4), 99 (Lightpoet), 102 (Vakalnick), 106 (Emanuele Leoni), 107 (Rui Vale De Sousa), 112 (Guiseppe Esposito), 113 (Luca Lorenzelli), 114 (Nikolay Antonov), 115 (BiancoBlue), 116 (Albiair), 117 (Dariya Maksimova), 118/119 (Eva Bocek), 128 (David Taljat), 129 (Julia Burlachenko), 133 (Rostislav Ageev), 134/135 (Ian Woolcock), 136 (Gutescu Eduard), 137 (Frimufilms), 139 top (Aliaksandr Mazurkevich), 139 bottom (Enigmaart), 148 (VanderWolfImages), 149 (Hel080808), 154/155 (Milton Cogheil), 158 (Paul Powici), 159 (Andrey Gudkov), 162 (Selle Mduda), 165 (Sergey Uryadnikov), 168 (Mrehssani), 170/171 (Matyas Rehak), 178 (Skouatroulio), 179 (Raindear4), 185 (Feelurroom), 188 (Letloose78), 191 (Youran Park), 194 (Lakhesis), 196/197 (Wirestock), 199 (Sean Pavone), 200 (Tawatchai Prakobkit), 201 (Musaiczbs), 202 (Steve Allen), 203 (Uditbatra1990), 204 (Ocusfocus), 205 (Szefei), 210 (Asif Himel), 213 top (Christopher Moswitzer), 214 (Chriskiely), 218 (Seadam), 219 (Itimages)

Getty Images: 63 (Tomas Zrna), 66 (Sascha Grabow), 152 (Education Images), 215 (Kieran Stone)

Shutterstock: 8 (Richard Cavalleri), 10 (eskystudio), 18/19 (Chase Clausen), 20 (dorinser), 21 (Jason Wilde), 22 (Andrew Gittis), 23 (Richard Cavalleri), 26 (Sean Lema), 27 (Yingna Cai), 30 & 31 (Rena Michael), 33 (Aneta Waberska), 34 (Pecold), 36 (Lukas Bischoff Photography), 37 (Robert Stolting), 38 (CCallanan), 39 (Oleg Kovtun Hydrobio), 41 (Kris Wiktor), 42/43 (Jason Stitt), 46 (Westtexasfish), 49 (James Pintar), 50 (Boris Vetshev), 51 (Porco-Rosso), 58 (SL-Photography), 60 (Ines Sacramento), 72 (Gonzalo Bunzoni), 73 (Yury Birukov), 80 (Marcin Kadziolka), 81 (Roland Zihlmann), 83, 84/85 (Michal Szymnski), 87 (Moian Adrian), 88/89 (Travelamos), 90 (Carlos IV Sequina), 92 (I Wei Huang), 95 (Gaspar Janos), 96 (travelpeter), 98 (Huang Zheng), 100 (Tomasz Czajkowski), 101 (Jon Chica), 103 (Sergio Michelini), 105 (Philippe 1 bo), 120 (Atmosphere1), 121 (Daliu), 122 (Boris Stroujko), 124/125 (Mike Mareen), 126 (Tomasz Warszewski), 127 (May_Lana), 130/131 (Hike The World), 132 (Przemyslaw Wasilewski), 138 (Piotr Piatrouski), 140/141 (vvvita), 142 (Ppictures), 144/145 (Natalya Bozadzhy), 146 left (Fotystory), 146 top right (Iapas77), 146 bottom right (Giampaolo Gianella), 150 (E Pasqualli), 151 (Pascale Gueret), 156/157 (Homo Cosmicos), 160/161 Dmussman, 163 (JT Platt), 164 (Sergey Uryadnikov), 172 (Sergey Dzuba), 173 (nikidel), 174 (Iryna Hromotska), 175 (Focus-Redefine-Fotography), 176 (OlegD), 177 (Waj), 180 (Dashu Xinganling), 181 (Weiming Xie), 182 (milezaway), 183 (David Webb), 184 (vichie81), 186 (Ulysses Ybiernan), 187 (Hiroshi Iha), 189 (Tappasan Phurisamrit), 190 (Hien Phung Thu), 192/193 (Nguyen Quang Ngoc Tonkin), 198 left (Christian Nuebling), 198 right (RooftopStudioBangkok), 209 (Altung Galip), 211 (Asia Travel), 212 (Marius Dobilas), 213 bottom (Dima Fadeer), 220/221 (Romaine W), 222/223 (Maridav)